In the Keep of Forgetting

In the Keep of Forgetting

Poems

W. N. Gates

SUNSTONE PRESS

SANTA FE

Sunstone books may be purchased for educational, business, or sales promotional use. For information please write: Special Markets Department, Sunstone Press, P.O. Box 2321, Santa Fe, New Mexico 87504-2321.

Book and cover design › R. Ahl
Printed on acid-free paper
∞

Library of Congress Cataloging-in-Publication Data

Names: Gates, William N., 1930- author.
Title: In the keep of forgetting : poems / William N. Gates.
Description: Santa Fe : Sunstone Press, [2021] | Summary: "A collection of poems from a well known Southwestern U.S. writer"-- Provided by publisher.
Identifiers: LCCN 2021002104 | ISBN 9781632933270 (paperback)
Subjects: LCGFT: Poetry.
Classification: LCC PS3607.A7888 I5 2021 | DDC 811/.6--dc23
LC record available at https://lccn.loc.gov/2021002104

WWW.SUNSTONEPRESS.COM
SUNSTONE PRESS / POST OFFICE BOX 2321 / SANTA FE, NM 87504-2321 /USA
(505) 988-4418 / FAX (505) 988-1025

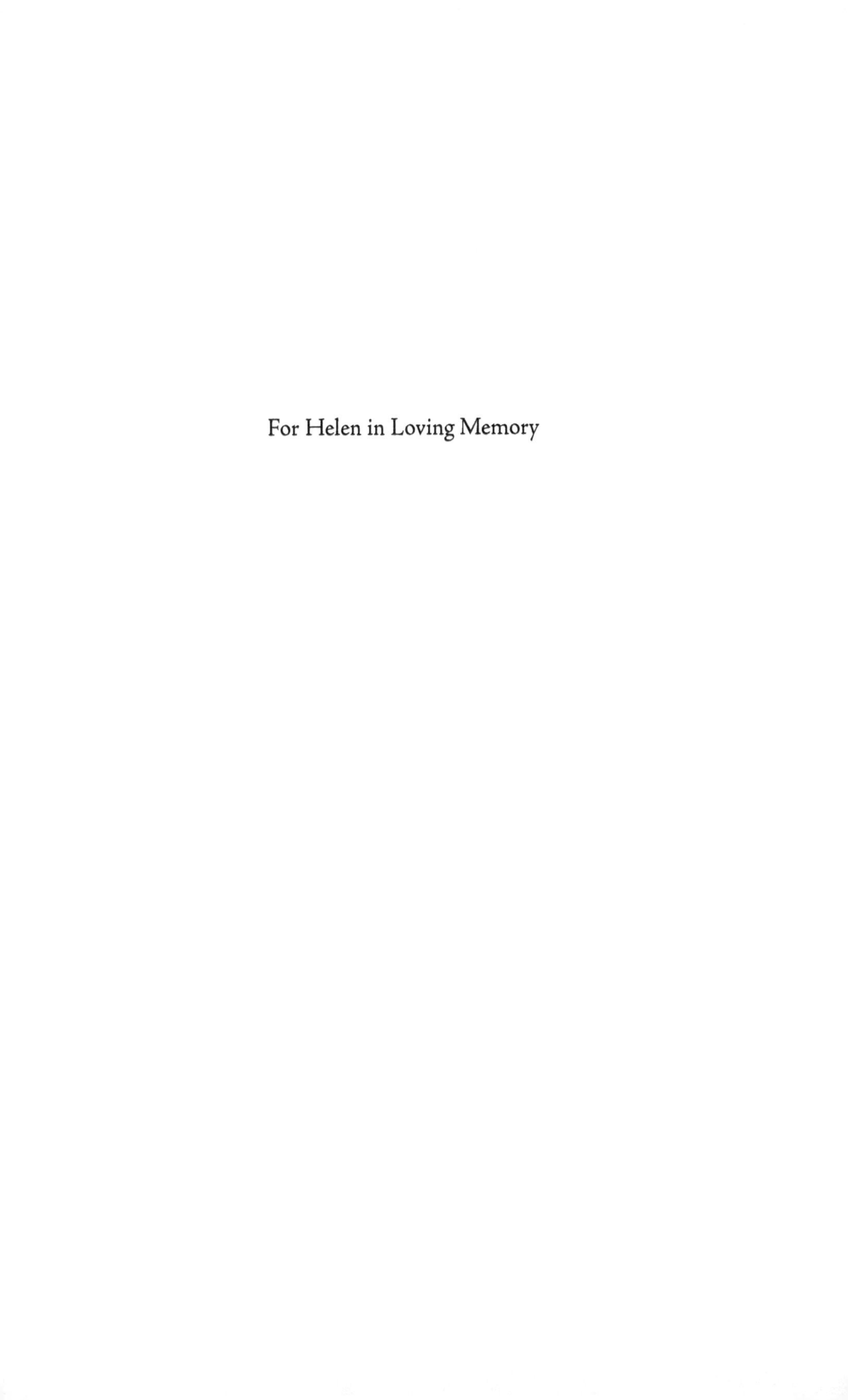

For Helen in Loving Memory

CONTENTS

PREFACE

Years ago, when Helen and I lived in Seattle, I invented a style of
rapid writing to which I set a strict limit of five minutes without stopping to
revise or punctuate, and leaving blank space for breath or pause. I put a clock
time at the start and at the end of each piece.

I believed these quick takes could stand on their own, and for a long
time they formed the main current of my work. I chose big sketch books
which gave me pure unlined paper to scribble upon with pen and pencil
rather than typewriter.

By 2014 I began to see this streamlined prose could be the seed and
sprout of poems. And in the following I offer the reader examples, first, of
the "quick take" and then the resulting "crafted poem." The quoted phrase in
the quick take is by Henry James.

July 12, 2010

9:32 her latest haircut revealing
lines of her neck upsweeping roots of tree
young tree young spruce beguiling my hand
that
wants to stroke tail of dark hair upsweeping
into dark & gray thickness elegant passage
of her nape & long neck to stroke is to desire
intimation of "present palpable intimate"
I sense it coming ah the back of her
neck to admire to stroke
9:37

On Her New
Haircut

Her hair,
New-bared, nape
Naked, upsweeping;
Invoked to stroke
My hand traced
One dark trail
Expanding upward
Into a mix,
Thick-soft-prickly
Ends' encounter,
In brushing, brushed;
So many points
Of lust provoked;
Empty envious
Hand must wander
Elsewhere on her.

POT OF PAPER-WHITES

Each bulb bursts,
Shoots its rocket,
Lofts long tendrils,
Parts its petals;
Soundless spree,
Silent crackle,
Then lean, droop,
Stalk, string,
Stick can't prop,
They want to sleep.

Spring Arranged
Dumbarton Oaks, Late March

From this high stage we overlook
The stone-carved water ovals; mosaic
Pebble sheaves of wheat; pools
Of clarity, a skin for any
Casual breeze to brush and prickle.

Down below, the terraced grass
Leads to cherry pinks amassed
Against a haze of winter woods.
We climb stepped paths to fountains
Blooming toward their grand collapse.

On through garden rooms enclosing
Reckless fading orange crocus,
Yellow-bonneted daffodils,
Where boxwood sows remembrance with
A peppery tang. Now is time

For self-possessed of buds to open,
Squander colors on the world.
Purple-white magnolia's languid
Easy-loosened petals fall.
Walking these mnemonic ways

I like to think of you at two,
Riding on your father's shoulders
To explore this singular spring,
So redolent of you. My love
Would claim you every stage of life.

Equinox

Buds tip magnolia tulip
Poplar sports tiny sprouts
Beech's hard dark darts
Split peer despite March
Ice relents rots reluctant
April chill clouds scudding
Dogwood reaches far feelers
Beaded redbuds brood bide
Forsythia fanfare foretells splurge
Explodes pear plum cherry
Varying verdure floral flux
Crabapple pink azalea vermilion
Watermelon madder magenta
Mango orange rhododendrons
Dusk darkens leaves flocks
Flowers fade spring spent
Sultry sullen summer comes

River, Ruled

Miles to west of city ways,
Hiking by an easy-going river,
We came upon a dam so proud
It stopped us short: a reservoir
Gorged, swollen so it stuffed
The booming central chute and even
Let the waters overbrim
The rim to slide in lacy sheets
Down slanted walls that ruled them
Horizontal like a page,
Ever written in a flux
Of white and fleeing script that chased
And overlapped in silent race
To feed and mend the river's way.
Despite itself that blockage
Made the moving waters write.
And we enchanted lovers turned
To wander back the way we came,
But looking back to see what seemed
Snowflakes falling through the trees,
And to hear what sounded like
The distant thumps of a marching band.

Longwood Gardens in May

Magenta rhododendron bundles
We caress, lingering along
Those allées; (fescue underfoot,
Blue-green, seeded stems, thin);
Admire the dainty Fringe Tree,
Fragrant, radiant as snow;

Crane our necks to scan high
Trunks of Tulip Poplar, harbors
For singing wood thrush; cardinals
Calling "tew tew tew tew"
In capitols of Catalpa, vaults
Of Copper Beech; on we wander

In the halls of barks and resins
Slowly seeping. Agog amid
Paragons of peony,
We're drawn away by shouts of children
Running to the water garden;
There we find a liquid street

Leading down low steps toward
A turret of white, pushing upward
Through its own falling, a clash
Of waters balancing before
Collapsing in their pool,
Sprinkling children in delight.

Spring Unbound

Now the new upstarts have pierced
The brown and ocher mishmash of old
Cold of autumn and before.
Soggy underfoot the trail
Curves by riverways, whose water
Feeds the roots of tulip trees
And receives them when they die;
Still some will block the trail so we
Must straddle over fallen trunks
Or trek the long way around to step
Across their tops. But detour gives us
Whiffs of roses, sprinkle of floral
Asterisks and thickets of laurel
With their tiny parasols
Sprigged with red. Overhead
The greens screen the lights of sky,
We walk captive in their cavern.
Circles, curls of river current,
Leaf-lights, zoom of flies and bees
Confuse our peering deep to find
The umber somber bottom stones,
Backbone of river, land and spring.

Oregano, parsley, mint,
Taragon, camomile, carraway—
Snugged in beds and borders,
They escape and fly away
Over fields, counties, countries,
Broadcast, bird-cast, windblown,
Vagabonds, volunteers they mingle
With Russian thistle tumbling,
Rolling disreputable
Bundles, briars, brambles,
Rambling blackberry jumbles.

Autumn Jays

"Here—here—here—"
They cried, wings whickering,
And lighted on the piñons
Gleaning, grabbing nuts,
Crackling as they jabbed
For last of crop (late
Comers, cones empty,
Nuts already nabbed);
The trees shook and swayed
Under their attack,
Upside down they hung
On bobbing twigs, lost hold,
Dropped, caught themselves,
Raced away pulling
One after another until
All flocked away crying
"Where—where—where—"

Blackbirds Foraging

Glimmering blue in black
With brilliant yellow eyes
They race through building gaps
Toward the street of beech-tree
Bronze where nuts are dropping,
Cracking, crushed by traffic,
Foragers' easy gorging;
They strut and screak and beak
Them up, gobble and glean
Until warned by a beep
They all fly up in a gust,
The inner wind that routs them,
Shoos them on to further chance.

An Emigration

Dreams follow through, flotsam drifting,
Then for one time only comes
A major iceberg, a frozen court
Peopled by an august noblesse
With flame-orange patches on their cheeks;
In black evening dress they gather,
Point their bills up and over
Each other's shoulders toward the far
Horizons, magnificent personages
On a white and blue-green palace
Come floating past, now cast off
From their imperial polar matrix
To find their fate in alien seas.

BEAR IN MOTION

Shaggy rusty boulderly bulk
Rears up to stand flat-footed;
Cats jump up to cuff and box,
Bear can ponderously walk,
A monument in motion, shoulders
Thrusting forward, cone and snout
Wiggling, sniffing sideways; drops
Down all fours to ground; gathers
Stride, forepaws, claws spread
To place, plash, advance (one
Swat can behead any man); paw
Withdraws, claws retract; all parts
Roll with supple heavy jiggling.
Thick rough hair hides tiny
Wary eyes, which when it stands
Can spy ahead whatever moves.
Yet its formidable hide cannot
Deflect the dope-dart that will
Knock it out for hauling to a zoo.

National Zoo Baby

Just born, four lank legs must lift
At once (two or three won't work),
Like stilts or wobbly tent poles, splay
Too wide and they collapse again.
Again to struggle, and to flop.
The lofty mother reaches down,
Nudges, licks with long black tongue.
Then the rickety infant's props
Tremble, stagger, stand, hold.
The human crowd sighs and cheers,
An Italian visitor cries "Ecco!
Viva la bella bambina giraffa!"
At that she takes a lurching step.

Along lawns juicy green
Black white silver flocking
Crows seagulls voices merging
Scratchy voices mothers talking
Ferry children park pathways
Walking yacking babies foods
Products Seattle nasal prattle
Trees shadow flat vowels
Silver black white squealing
Squawking flap flutter winging
Landing folding feathers pecking
Poking black silver white

OCTOBER OUTLOOK

I hear the low chant
Of shorn sharp aspen
Whipping the wind;
The sky's clear deep blue,
The valley of tawny earth
Tinged by cottonwood
And yellow chamisa leads
On to the far mountains
That look so near.

May these trees survive
Once more the caterpillar swarms
That ravage them, and once
More regenerate their greens.
How it chills and forebodes,
The chant of the shorn.

Climbing

I saw them climbing from below,
The conifers, fir and ponderosa,
They overtook me on the trail
To heights I couldn't see.

In answer to a minor wind
They sang an old susurrus hymn
And lifted me along with them.
I was younger then and bound

To find out what was uppermost,
And by step over step I found
Where firs gave way to aspen groves
And shooting stars and columbines,

And on beyond, the spears of spruce
Pointing up to timberline,
And from there all rock with lichen
Green and gray, and squeaks of pika:

Boulders built on boulders, no more
Except enormous breathing blue,
Beyond belief or depth complete
With an occasional shred of cloud.

It seemed the peaks, the trees, the flowers
Were in procession, waiting in
Attendance on that sky for whatever
It would bring. I found I was alone

And yet not lonely; I would not
Be lost because the one way back
Led down the path that I had climbed;
The only hazard was to fall
But that lay years beyond surmise.

Mid-Life Hike

We entered changing aspen,
Saw their shivering leaves,
Lemon yellows tingling
Where they teased the blue
Which darkened in response.
A couple's different natures
Provoke a clash of colors;
Nature kept us lusty;
Had no use for aging,
Would strip us like the leaves;
Yet near the cruel end
We knew we'd had it all.

Ponderosa Downed

Deep in forest, unregarded,
Bound to ground with no escape,
The pillar of a pine has fallen.
Bare of bark, lightning-charred,
Once looked-up-to, tackling winds,
Is now thrown down and prone to rest.
Its sinuous limbs are snapped and scattered,
Its spire intact, reptilian spear
Now close that was too far aloft
To see.

        The heartwood core endures
Cushioned in its own pine straw,
The pliant quills in clasps of three,
Ponderosa pen-strokes layered
Ocher rust above gray and black,
Springy bed for sun to bake.
Now begins the slow smolder,
Moldering to make more earth.

And this the quiet aftermath,
For who has ever seen or heard
The like of such a grounding crash
But wind the pusher and the witness.

So Long Until Then

Through the windshield
Low overcast,
Maidenly aspens
Waving sadly
Goodbye until then,
Raindrops pat,
Moue, merge, blur
The wide-eyed glass,
Deform the leafy girls
Swaying in teary wind,
They drowsily flutter
Desponding, glass now
One sliding film
Dissolving all,
Poor day,
Last day to walk,
So long until then.

Piñons pining
Forlorn despond
Mourn bowed
Down boughs
Burdened borne
Ponderous mitts
Wet glut

Morning mends
Snows snooze
Bough sloughs
Springs free
Solemn nodding
Wad by wad
Trees agree
Bow sedately
Stately

Swing Time

The trombones bow as one,
Swing up and point to the moon,
The crooning saxes surge
And sway from side to side,
The man with wavy shiny hair
Moseys up and sings,
"Step aside partner, it's my day"
And the saxophones chant,
"deeoodlyoop, deeoodlyoop-ah"

Blessed swing-time U.S.A.,
Our day for each and all;
Eleanor Roosevelt writes
"My Day" for years while years
Fly by like shades escaping
Faster and faster and
Roll up with a whack.
Yet a moment can swell and dwell
On a mood of winter morning,
With snow to suck or pack,
Whistle of corduroys
Swiping together, slightly
Off the beat of footfalls.

Looking Backward

Then we looked down upon the tiny
Toilsome trails that crawled the land
We'd crossed like ants, now embraced
In one survey out free of trees;
As if winged, or astride a giant
Horse of steep mountain ridge
That led us higher, clear to see
Everywhere we'd crept or stepped
Down deep in wider wilderness,
To the streaming watershed
And fragile lake concealed beyond
Entanglements of evergreen.

Europe, 1919

To fill in the missing parts,
Special masks of their former faces
Were fitted so they could go
Outside in public places
Like ordinary men in hats,
Old suits and vests and stiff
White collars and cravats.

A worn-out, starved and hollowed
People took back their sons,
However hacked or hobbling
Or down on stumps, holding out
A cup for worthless coins.

That war would fix the future
Lifetimes of their children
And their children's children,
Since war has generative power:
As One begat Two, Two begat Three
And Three begat Four, and counting.

Playing Dead

As kids they called it "playing dead"
And dueled with sticks and clashed for entry,
For touchés and mortal jabs;
Claiming kills they hopped and feinted,
Eyes ever on opposing points.
Next they drew their pseudo Lugers,
Aimed imaginary Brownings,
Yelled "I got you," and unless
He argued, he would topple
Picturesquely to the ground,
Such was the game in '41.

THE CORNFIELD, 1939

Once in, deep in, he'd lose
Himself and disappear
In rows of trusty stalks
With tassels high above,
The dry consoling whisper
Of lank and floppy leaves
And scent of swelling cobs
In tight green purses, refuge
For a runaway child
Needing to mourn by himself.

Just Suppose

Just suppose, juxtaposed,
Side by side or sliding one
Above the other: cased in glass,
Consoling calm of celadon
From an ancient dynasty
A pale bowl sage green,
Tinged with copper to infuse
Deep carmine in the green –

Inside a P-47, all guns jerking,
Shaky movie gulping, rushing
Over tree-tops, sighting
Road, truck, train
As a flat laconic voice tells
What's jolting through his cockpit,
Blobs, blurs and tracer dots
Toward a vague shape exploding –

How we receive and hold them both,
Side by side, or one
Imposed upon the other.

In Memoriam

A sunny day we crossed the street
To see that black plow of stone
Delving into earth, where people
Were descending to the names
So lightly cut and faint to read.

I said to Marian, "Strange to be here,
We who worked so hard against it."
She: "That's not to do with these
Who never should have gone." Then why
Come here? Not just to look

Or in some way to tabulate
The grief we'd struggled to prevent.
In our way we too were veterans,
Waking every bitter morning
To the nightmare of our country.

And here were those who died in it.
Marian, old friend, so tall and lame
She had to sidle down the ramp,
But go she would as she had vowed.
Marian, John, Nat and Lu,

Jim and Blythe, Bill and Ann,
Names among the many who
Defied not just the powers that were,
But all who temporized, or closed
Their eyes, or were indifferent.

Bach, Unaccompanied

Lone
Man, violin,
Sonata solo,
Bare aria,
His foot starts
To beat, to pace

Here, there,
Down stepped
Harmonic stairs
In phrases praising;
A bowstring breaks,
Waves above –

Sostenuto,
Grave, grieving,
Long-drawn chords,
Thirds in one stroke,
A triad in one,
Four in one –

Finale, fast,
Lost bowstrings
Whip and whirl;
As insects spinning
He spurs his notes
In a blur of bowing –

Slowed, sown;
Man wan, worn;
Stops, stoops;
Muse, music, man
Interfused,
Done.

Three Day Pass
    Christmas 1952

We jammed into one hotel room,
Got drunk on cocktails mixed
In the waste pail with a hanger,
Closed in to flirt and dance
With the two available wives.

GI's I knew aimed to get
A job, marriage, kids,
The safe and popular future.
Ignorant I dreamed of love
Though love involved confusion –
Botticelli, lemon pie,
Audrey Hepburn,
Mozart's 41st,
Benny Goodman Trio's
"Body and Soul,"
Mary Lou Williams'
"Little Joe From Chicago."

Whatever lay in wait for us,
Lovers we must be
As well as soldiers, killers,
Voters, husbands, daddies,
All-around citizens and studs.
Years later a friend lamented,
"Love died" – Eros slowly
Nibbled and gnawed to death
By one thing and another.

My disbelief would melt in you.
You said, "You write because
You love"; and writing

Was a way to celebrate
The whole round world of sound,
Feel, smell, taste, sight;
And you were its angel
And its body I could love
In words as well as silence.

BRITTEN'S FIRST QUARTET
(OPUS 25 IN D-MAJOR)

What in the world or sky, such marvel,
The Andante Sostenuto, high as prevailing
Loftiest winds, the extreme treble
Of strings in trio accented by plucks
Of cello, as the four flew ethereal
Space-wide sweeps. Remembered, kept
In mind many years, now in skilled
Hands played once again, the sound
Of cirrus strokes across blue,
Their tenuous force streams beyond ken.
      Composed in 1941, in exile,
        His homeland being blitzed from above.

In Memoriam,
Benjamin Britten,
1913—1976

Impromptu by Schubert

Enclosed by trucks, buses,
Confused and scuffling cars,
I swim on a wave of cantabile,
Fins of music glide me
Through all the push and racket
To a market parking place
And hold me in a trance
I cannot interrupt.
Even inside the store
The chords companion me,
Vying with piles of products,
Never to be lost.

Enduring Apparitions

A crackle of ice betrays
The creep of a car outside,
In a dark daybreak awake
In my traffic of memory,
1960 – '45 – '70 –
Wars – JFK – not
So long ago but a long
Erosion punctured by shocks,
Now gone, no more youth,
Kennedys, marriage, divorce,
Save in ongoing chatter
Of memory, or in aspects
Of grownup children beside
Their photos as they were:

Double image to solve,
The child of three,
Easter, '67,
In her best spring dress,
Ages distant from present
City towers dawning
In the picture glass,
She clasps the chains of a swing,
Her hands, cheeks, nose
Still round, her short hair
Mussed by a gentle wind,
Her lips and eyes in wonder
At whatever could come next.

Then the boy of six,
Also blurred by glass,
Momently still, musing
On pteranodons,

Profile traced in touches
Of hair, brow, nose
Delicately sharp
Despite the jangle of times.

Then the girl of nine
Smiling past her shoulder,
Her new front teeth,
Her delighted eyes
On someone out of sight, and light
Catching on a braid
And pills of woolen sweater,
She learns the jumble of time.

I needed them as much
As they needed me; love
Cannot go without saying.

DIRECTIVE

Alphabet's the keyboard:
Reciting consonants to hook
A vowel, or voicing vowels
To fit a consonant,
And fingering these scales
With hunger and élan:
Long – lung – languor –
Tongue – tang – tingle –
Slunk – sunk – stunk –
Be a player of letters,
Make a poem be the music
And the dance of words.

To Go To Sleep

You must hush,
Crush your voices,
Push away mutters
Of daily matters,
Breathe as taught:
Long inhale,
Long exhale,
Long incoming,
Long withdraw,
A suave shore,
Not roars of storm,
Agreeable sea
Lapping, sipping
At its margins,
After raging,
Ravaging houses
Playing now
Soft as cats.

FLUX

Jet stream supreme
Speeding seamless,
Memory clocks,
Locks moment,
Years blur,
Flown forgotten.
Clouds flow,
Glowing towns,
Snowflakes sown
Sleep deep.
Sunrise surprise,
City silenced.
Plow shoves
Downy mountain,
Shovels chop,
Scrape heaps,
Ranges wane,
Rains ruin;
Sodden clods,
Charm shamed,
Draggle,
Drab.

Refuge

You outdoors who cringe and shiver
In freezing fog or sleet,
Come into a healing mist
That will permeate your pores,
Breathe giant tender fronds,
Ferns as tall as trees
With ginger winding round them,
Birds of paradise that bloom
With blue and orange beak and plumes;
All sheltered under vaulted glass
That overtops the tallest;
One step within, your sighs will rise
In sensual shock delicious as
Hot soup or face-cloth to the eyes;
Your ears will catch, in lives
Timed to the minute, the slow
Clock of drops pent.

Daybreak

Chasing sour thought
Sun streaks in and probes
Cassette, cup, pencil,
Transforms a crumpled paper,
Revels in a glass,
Caroms billiard-like
Across the ceiling down
The wall to floor,
Deflecting serious thought.

Morning Greetings

When wave slams against rock and up,
And cloud towers up, spreading wings,
Radiant wipes, plucked from a box
Stand arrested, superb in sunlight,
Greeting us all with a gesture.

The Hiss of Sand

Hear hiss of sand embraced
By farthest lunge of wave,
Voracious kiss of massed grains
Pushed, pressed, sucked away,
Foam and grist glistening
In their mix; but in no time
The sequent brute rears,
Tilts tossing toward
Its ravishment.

Dream

"Go Fiona" called her friend
As we stepped onto ice
And skated as one, my left arm
Around her, hands joined across,
I dipped my right leg, pushed us forth
Among tables and skaters, between
And around in a long yearning circle;
Once I caught her up, held her
Cradled in my arms (she grew
Very small), even as children
We'd have charmed one another;
No past, no future, with occasional
Right-side dips to propel us
Along in figures we made,
Our enchantment was
The continuing moment.

We took a wooded path
Through a parenthetic park
Across city streets
Until construction barred us:
Crane, bulldozer, trucks,
Backhoe gobbling earth;
But when we slipped between,
Pushed on a little way,
Even through that din
We caught the call of wood thrush,
Its precise repeated chant
And then a flourish, insisting
On song amid chaos.

SEQUENCE

So pleased to be between you two
That I'd forgot some thing I must
Retrieve, and so I left and back-
Tracked to the bus—one way, eight dollars—
Back to where we'd been, inside
To find whatever I had left,
And to finish shaving;
Again entangled in a dream
Which only meant to catch me up
In convolutions leading on
To scenes more trifling and compelling;

But then a train blared harmonious
Cheer and pulled me out of sleep
To listen to that toot receding,
Introducing a duet of doves
That coo'd a half-tone out of tune.

Maryland Leaf Watch

Within a hazy mile of range
These venerable mountains show
Their tapestries before they fade
Toward the city to the east.

Easy, swinging up a mile
Off-road, that Catoctin trail
Lifts us in a slow wave
Up and over boulders, presents

To us the sumptuous forest trash
Of sassafras and tulip, tupelo and oak,
Sycamore and maple, saffron, umber,
Hazel, crimson, bronze, their smell

Overlapping past and present,
Rich man, poor man, on display
For a day or pressed in a book,
Preserved arid, frail, intact.

DECEMBER BELLS

Bong   Bring   Brung
    Brung   Brong   Bong
        Born   Born   Born

            Down step
            Timed
            Tones ears
            Astound
            Windows wide
            Hear
            Declare rare
            Airs
            Profound deep
            Tongues
            Bells compel
            Well—
            Come bring
            Boon
            Over come
            Dull
            Hum drum
            Town

Dreams of Going Away

Before departing I released
All belongings, works, paintings,
One, a sinuous nude in cool
Blue-green which I picked up
And showed the people gathered there.
All the rest, the etcetera,
Tossed and piled in one reproachful
Sullen mass I would forsake,
For I was going somewhere
I did not know,
But I must go.

Dreaming of New Mexico From Far Away

Soon we'll be up there,
Where waters swollen strong
Come streaming down tumbled
Rocks and thwarts of log,
But parenthetic swerves
Allow an islet colony
Of columbines' capacious
Bonnets blue and white
With long spurs nodding,
That only needling beak
Of hummingbird can probe
To find and drink the nectar –

Soon we'll be out of here
And on our way up there.

SPRING, CREEKSIDE

A bump of stone is marking time,
Every other sound's immersed
In present rushing, up ahead
The future, to be, to come
Head-on toward you, by you,
Gone for all its worth
This way, that way, out of sight,
Lavish giveaway of time
Marked by muffled thumps of rock
With odd, syncopated offbeats.

"Oh, It's You"

I fumble for a name to fit
The ancient face and voice that calls
As I walk downtown beside
Acequia Madre, the Mother Ditch,
Past refashioned old adobes,
High walls, hidden retreats.

Not the neighborhood that was,
Now mainly for the well-to-do,
Plaque'd 'worthy of preservation,'
With impenetrable gates
And Mother Ditch a kind of moat
That one time watered corn and beans.

"So it is you – you here to stay?"
My ghosts are rattling their chains,
Names I must and will not lose:
Hello, Ginger; hello, Brad;
Hi, Susan, Booker; Tom and Paula;
Dave and Patty; hello, Elinore –

So often left but then remembered.
Shall we settle in this place,
Old people searching for a final
Residence for good or ill;
Maybe it'll be the clasp
Of resonance will keep us here.

They kneel to strike the match
And make the only light to warm them,
Flame snatches paper, sticks,
Which disappear up–chimney but
Their log has caught and settles
To a steady gnawing. Their eyes
Enamored of the fire do not see
The silent ceiling play above
Of giant shadows dodging,
Grappling with the light;
They crouch to embrace their sinking wood,
Now in coals and embers dwindling
To a hiss and tick; their skins
And hearts entreat retreating heat.

Jet stream encircling the world,
Meteor trails of sparkling dust,
Rapids of thought, winter clouds
Reflecting city glow – even
Marmoreal memories dissolve,
Nothing seems to hold except
A long-forgotten face and hat
That fit a long-forgotten voice,
Then only the tone or timbre, hardly
A scrap of what they're telling us.

Relationships

Bend, bind,
Bond,
Twisted searching
Strands,
How they recoil
From one
Another, torn
Away
To droop, grope
Tangle,
Again to curl,
Catch,
Cling a while,
Then snap
In tortuous growth,
Trusting,
Detesting, shrinking
In devious
Fight for nurture,
Bound
To strive or escape –

Yet bound to vestiges
Of self who seem more shade
Than figure, not torn away
But outgrown, dispelled
When by chance one tendril
Finds another and they cling
And hug for good and all.

WHEN WE BEGAN

When we began,
Conspiring by phone,
Her timbre persuaded,
Her sound salved regret,
Awoke moist molecules,
Dissolved the old life.

On Her New Haircut

Her hair,
New-bared, nape
Naked, upsweeping;
Invoked to stroke
My hand traced
One dark trail
Expanding upward
Into a mix,
Thick soft prickly
Ends' encounter,
In brushing, brushed;
So many points
Of lust provoked;
Empty envious
Hand must wander
Elsewhere on her.

Enticements

That night you lay along the sofa
Reading, flexing your toes
Which caught and fixed my sight
On those curves contracting, relaxing,
Plus an instep spectacularly deep
And featly footing –

That night I tried to read a book
While out of nowhere came
Your undulating sigh intending
Nothing special, just a passing
Moan, which pricked me up
And whetted my intent –

That night we lit a tall candle
In a tall and stately candle stick
And the light was not too bright
And not too dim to bathe us in it.

Trust in Love

When sometimes I feel
The weight of sour self,
The weary sinkers, boredom,
Fret and alienation,

I chance to think of you,
Who raised me out of that
And gave to me a strange
New life of trust in love,

A drive to feed, a need
For you to seize my love
As food I cook for you;
No crutch, but something dire,

Requiring night and day
The touch of hands or feet;
And when, my obstacle,
You check my going somewhere,

Your body blocking me,
How can I resist
But squeeze the self of you?
I need a rosary,

Each bead a word from you
To pull me straight and supple
When I get out of sorts
And in an alien decline.

Luminous Teaching

Just past the autumnal equinox the sun
Will seize a brazen candlestick and play
Its offshoots in flamboyant rings across
A wall, or titillate a square glass vase,
Prolong its rays in prongs of blue and silver
And charm you so you shout for me to come.
Busy I may be but I have learned
To heed your teaching, sun and you are so
Intriguing.

A January Gift

Chilled, tired we sat and read
Our books beside the big glass door
That framed the last of western sun
Which in its setting caught, by jut
Of roof, a giant icicle,
Illumined all its hard and lustrous
In's and out's, and tapped the wall
With soft O's of red-gold ocher,
And reaching in to us revealed
The incandescence of mahogany.

To Be So Dull

To be so dull or blind
Or bored or in a rage
To get somewhere that one
Would miss that sycamore
Dancing in a dale,
Crooked-branching Shiva
Prancing on one foot;
Its motley bark was patched
In pale green and blue,
It made a room for itself
Amid a grove of others.
And when you called to look
I slowed and paused for seconds
Despite a car blaring
At us from behind.

In The Keep of Forgetting

As if one impulse took from another
And hid and kept safe from theft and her
Recalling, she could not solve the loss
Of the treasure which, as years would pass
And fade, she grieved someone had stolen.

And now when packing to move away
Every cubbyhole must be emptied;
And from a cupboard they pulled a jumble
Of bags, and in one bag a flannel
Packet, and in that packet found
And poured out more and more precious
Glistening ropes of the sea-born Murano
Necklace woven of tiny gems,
Held close in the keep of forgetting.

II

She's always there, close as touch
And far as the moon, behind blinds
Of duties and diurnal distractions,
Push them aside, pull her close,
How could he forget. No more.
Time rushes on, she's right there.

"My molecules have changed," she says
Lazing in molten molecular
Splendor. The triumph of desire
Vanishes yet stays to sway,
To sweep all else away.

Old Timers' Drink Time

Clink time
Nears bearing
Cheering chimes
Lemon strip
Piquant sip
Tongue tingles
Elates palate
Martini taps
Cotes du Rhone
Together ring
We gather in
To one another
Brink time
Age engaged
Assuaged